Slumber Party Book

DOUGLAS LOVE
Pictures by Marty Norman

A Beech Tree Paperback Book
New York

The text type is Palatino.

Library of Congress Cataloging in Publication Data
Love, Douglas.
Slumber party book / by Douglas Love ; illustrated by Marty Norman.
p. cm.
Summary: Provides ideas for slumber parties on nine different themes,
covering everything from invitations, activities, food, and favors.
1. Children's parties—Juvenile literature.
2. Sleepovers—Juvenile literature. 3. Amusements—Juvenile literature.
[1. Parties 2. Birthdays. 3. Sleepovers.] I. Norman, Marty, 1934–   ill. II. Title.
GV1205.L69 1997 96-41807 CIP AC
ISBN 0-688-15259-7

1 3 5 7 9 10 8 6 4 2
First Edition

For Cecily

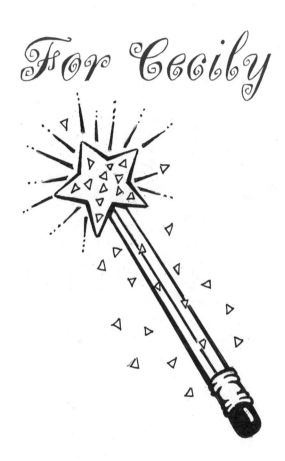

Contents

Introduction

* *

Think of all the reasons you have to celebrate: Halloween, the opening of the school play, Groundhog Day, the last day of school, or your birthday. There's always a great reason to have a party—and you're old enough to plan your own special night and make it just what you want it to be.

Every chapter is a complete party. Each comes with illustrated plans for every aspect of your ultimate celebration, including invitations, decorations, games, recipes, activities, and favors. Near the end of the book you'll find some suggestions for cakes and breakfasts. You can follow one chapter or take different ideas from several to create your own unique bash. Plus, use the Memory Book pull-out in back to record your thoughts and paste pictures of your special party.

Each section of the book still needs your special touch and personal preferences. Add balloons and streamers to the suggested theme-oriented decorations, for example, or add your favorite dishes to the suggested recipes.

Remember, it's your party—make the most of it! Plan in advance. You will probably need to sit down with your parents and get the basic rules of the night out of the way. Take the time to find out what you can and cannot do, how many friends you can invite, and what time you have to pretend to go to sleep.

DON'T FORGET:

- Load a camera with film, and check the batteries on your camcorder to record the event.
- Remind each guest to bring her own sleeping bag and a plain pillowcase for everybody to autograph in indelible marker as a keepsake.
- *Make sure you get your parents' help or permission for all cooking in the kitchen!*

Be sure to get plenty of sleep the night before, because you and your friends will be having too much fun to close your eyes!

The Makeover Party

This is the night to try some fun new looks! What would it be like to look completely different from the way you do now? Do you think people would recognize you? Without making any permanent changes, have fun at this party, experimenting with makeup, nail polish, and hairstyles! This party takes some preparation, but it's worth it!

It's fun to play around with the way you look—as long as you make sure that you can go back to looking like yourself again. The main activity at this party will be makeovers of each of your guests. First, they will have a chance to try out different types of makeup. Decide if you'll supply the makeup or ask your friends to bring their own. They may choose to paint wild colors on their faces or enhance their own natural beauty with light touches.

If you are going to change your look, change it right down to your fingernails. It's fun to share your favorite nail designs. Next, give your guests an opportunity to try out new hairstyles and learn new techniques. Do you know how to create a French braid? Now's the time to teach your friends!

Mirrored invitations that you make yourself, a fashion-collage tablecloth, and delicious veggie dip and fruit salad round out this fantasy glamour celebration. Everyone gets a ribbon-covered hanger as a party favor to take home!

Invitations

It's a makeover sleep-over at Darcy's house! Bring your sleeping bag, hair ribbons, bows, barrettes, brushes, and an old shirt to: 123 Elm Street, Friday, April 3, at 6:00 P.M. RSVP 555-5555

HERE'S WHAT YOU NEED:

- Tagboard or thick card-stock paper
- Tinfoil
- Colored paper (pastel)
- Scissors and white glue
- Plastic tape (black or another color of your choice)
- Envelopes

Here's what you do:

- Use a pencil to draw the outline of a hand mirror on your tagboard.
- Carefully cut out the form with your scissors.
- Cover the round part of the tagboard with tinfoil, securing the edges to the back of your invitation with glue. Make sure that the foil faces shiny side up, and carefully smooth the surface with your thumb tip! Don't use too much foil, or the invite won't fit in an envelope.
- Cut a circle from the pastel paper, to cover the back of your mirror where you glued down the foil.
- Write all the party information on the pastel circle, and glue it to the back of the mirror.
- Take small strips of the colored plastic tape, and tape the edges of the circle, making a border.
- Tape around the handle of the mirror.
- Address envelopes and distribute to your friends!

Decorations

• •

Fashion Collage Tablecloth

If you have a lot of old magazines, you can create a collage decoration that will bring the party's theme to the food table.

Here's what you need:

- Old magazines
- A disposable paper tablecloth
- Scissors and glue

Here's what you do:

- Cut out pictures of models from old magazine ads.
- Start at the center of the tablecloth and glue overlapping cut-out figures directly on the paper.
- Your collage can cover just the center area of the table, or can extend to the corners of the paper.

Munchies

• •

High fashion can help a person look good. Healthy food makes you feel great on the inside *and* the outside. What is your favorite healthy recipe? Fresh fruits and vegetables not only taste delicious, they give your skin an inner glow that makeup could never duplicate.

Here's a raw vegetable dip and a fresh fruit salad to add zip to your fashion plates:

Veggie Dip

This dip recipe adds delicious flavor to any raw vegetable. Mix up a lot, because you'll run out fast!

Here's what you need:

- ½ cup mayonnaise or light mayonnaise
- 1½ cups sour cream or light sour cream or plain yogurt
- 3 tablespoons minced onions
- 1 tablespoon chopped or dried dill
- 1 teaspoon garlic salt
- ⅛ teaspoon black pepper
- Raw carrots
- Raw celery
- Red and/or green peppers

Great tasting food deserves a great presentation. Choose your serving dishes to complement the colors in your food. Feel free to decorate your platters with lettuce, orange slices, or fresh flowers!

FRUIT SALAD WITH YOGURT DRESSING

HERE'S WHAT YOU NEED:

- 2 cups each of your five favorite fruits (for example: grapes, oranges, apples, bananas, watermelon)
- 1 cup plain yogurt
- 2 teaspoons lemon juice
- 3 tablespoons honey

HERE'S WHAT YOU DO:

- In a bowl, mix the mayonnaise and sour cream or yogurt until well blended.
- Add the onions and dill. Mix thoroughly.
- Season with garlic salt and black pepper, to taste.
- Wash the carrots, celery, and peppers. Cut them into strips that are ¼ inch thick and 3 inches long.
- Arrange the raw vegetables on a platter in a circular pattern, alternating the colors around a small bowl of the white dip.
- Serves eight.

HERE'S WHAT YOU DO:

- Peel, seed, and slice your fruits into bite-sized pieces, and toss together in a large bowl.
- In a medium bowl, mix the yogurt, lemon juice, and honey until well blended.
- Toss fruit with dressing.
- Refrigerate. Serves eight.

MORE MENU SUGGESTIONS

Serve the Camera Cake or Center Stage Cake for dessert. (See recipes on pages 65 and 68.) For breakfast, granola with fresh fruit is the healthy choice.

The Party

. . . .

There are three major components to any makeover—makeup, nails, and hair. Before the party, make sure you're fully stocked with all your supplies. Split up your guests, and have everyone take turns making over and being made over.

> *Check all of your makeover products with an adult, to be sure that everything is safe and not permanent.*

Here are some ideas for each of your makeover stations:

MAKEUP

This is a good station to start your makeover process. Make sure you begin with a clean face and that there is a face cloth and a soap available for each guest. Have plenty of clips handy to hold hair out of your face while applying makeup.

Although too much makeup can cover up a girl's natural beauty, tonight is the time to go crazy and experiment. The make-up you put on each other at this party can be silly and just for fun. Have plenty of sponge applicators, tissues, cotton balls, and cotton swabs, so you won't have to share. Encourage your friends to share their talents and the tricks that they have learned about makeup.

Make a plan before you begin. Select a magazine ad or photograph for inspiration. Try to figure out what the model is wearing on her face before you begin to put makeup on yours.

Here are a few more tips to keep in mind during your makeover:

- Select colors that complement your natural coloring.
- Blend makeup in an upward motion with a cotton ball or your fingers, moving toward the hairline.
- Apply the makeup sparingly, so that it does not clump together.
- Keep plenty of wastebaskets around to discard tissues and swabs.
- Do not share applicators. Keep everything clean and sanitary.
- Don't fall asleep wearing your makeup. Your pillow will never forgive you!

Don't forget to use makeup that is hypoallergenic. You don't want any of your guests breaking out in purple spots!

NAILS

You can also add special nail designs and polish to your overall look. Be careful not to spill. Cover your work surface with plastic, and have plenty of remover and cotton balls available if you mess up. Many stores sell decal stickers, neon colors, and glitter polish that could be fun for this night of experimenting.

HAIR

Whether their hair is curly, straight, or wavy, dark, light, or red, your guests will have a ball discovering new styles that they can create for themselves or for each other.

Assemble clean brushes, combs, clips, barrettes, ribbons, curlers, curling irons, blow-dryers, styling gel, mousse, hair spray, and any other hair accessory you can think of. There are also sprays that change your hair color, but wash out completely. You might want to ask your friends to bring some of their own supplies to share.

Remember to have shampoo and conditioner available, just in case you run into a hair disaster. No one wants a bad-hair day at a makeover party!

Here are some tips to keep in mind as you transform:

- If you have long hair, try putting it up in a bun with a barrette or hairpins.
- If your hair is straight, try wetting it and adding gel. Before the gel dries, use a curling iron or rollers to give you instant curls!

Curling irons can get very hot! Make sure that you have an adult around to help out, or skip the iron and use sponge curlers and a blow-dryer.

- Try a new way of braiding your hair. If you know some braiding tricks, share them with your friends! Have you ever braided a ribbon right into your hair? Separate the hair you want to braid into two sections, using the ribbon as the third, and braid as usual for a pretty, new look.
- Slick your hair back with gel and a comb for an elegant and glamorous look.
- Have a bunch of hand mirrors available so you can see both front and back while you are working!

FASHION MOBILE

Ready to hit the runway? This is a great use for all those magazines you have lying around your house before they hit the recycling bin. Let each guest choose five favorite styles to highlight her new look.

HERE'S WHAT YOU NEED:

- Old magazines
- Wire hangers
- Construction paper
- Thick ribbon
- Thin ribbon or colored string
- Scissors, glue, and a hole punch

<u>HERE'S WHAT YOU DO:</u>

- Cover each hanger with thick ribbon by tying the end to the hook, and then wrapping the ribbon around and around until none of the wire is showing. Tie the other end with a knot and clip off the edges.
- Have everyone page through old magazines and clip out pictures of fun fashions that catch her eye.
- Carefully cut around the figure in the magazine.
- Glue the figure to the construction paper, then trim the paper to the size and shape of the magazine figure. Leave a ¾-inch tab at the top of the construction paper.
- Punch a hole in the tab for string to go through.
- Once you have created five or six figures, cut your string to varying lengths and tie your figures to your hanger.
- When your guests leave the next morning, their hanger mobiles will make great party favors. The ribbon-covered hangers won't stretch out their favorite fashions.

Show off your new looks for the camera! You'll want lots of pictures and great memories of this special celebration!

The Hollywood Party

It's glamorous and exciting—it's Hollywood! The color scheme for the entire party is black and white. Everything will be black and white: invitations, decorations, maybe even the cake. What do you have to wear that's black and white?

The theme is set with your invitations in the shape of a black-and-white movie marquee. The sidewalk outside your house will be decorated with Walk-of-Fame stars.

Have you ever thought about what it would be like to star in a movie? Tonight's feature presentation is your favorite movie classic followed by a live reenactment. You and your guests will have a chance to act out your favorite scenes.

Flavored popcorn is the snack highlight of the party, served in cones that you make yourself, while you munch on star sandwiches. You and your guests will be calling "Lights! Camera! Action!" before the night is through!

Invitations

Modeled after a movie marquee, this black-and-white invitation with silver glitter clearly states the theme of the party and asks your guests to come prepared!

It's a black-and-white Hollywood
sleep-over at Lauren's!
Come dressed in black and white for
celebrity games and movie classics.
123 Elm Street, Saturday, August 29, at 6:00 P.M.
RSVP 555-5555

- Black construction paper
- Plain white paper (8½ x 11 inches)
- Scissors, glue, and a hole punch
- Black marker
- A shoe box
- Silver glitter
- Envelopes

HERE'S WHAT YOU DO:

- Cut the white paper into 4¼- x 5½-inch rectangles
- Cut half-inch strips of black paper
- Punch holes evenly in the black strips, leaving ⅛-inch spaces between the holes.
- Glue the strips to the edges of the white rectangles, creating a border or frame.

- Use the black marker to write your party information on the white paper within the black borders.
- Place a line of glue at the edge of each of the four black borders.
- Before the glue dries, place the invitation into a shoe box and sprinkle with silver glitter. Shake the excess into the box.
- Allow invitations to dry overnight.
- Mail or give to your friends.

Decorations and Favors

Remember, it's black-and-white night! Use only black-and-white balloons and streamers. For extra flare, use touches of silver. But don't stop there! Use black-and-white plates, napkins, tablecloths, forks, and knives. Be creative without color!

WALK OF FAME

- Use chalk to draw stars on the sidewalk or driveway in front of your house.
- In the center of the stars, write the names of your favorite actors or the names of your guests.
- If your party starts after the sun goes down, the Walk of Fame will be a surprise for your guests when they leave the next morning!

BLACK-AND-WHITE POPCORN CONES

You can't watch movies without popcorn! Everyone gets her own popcorn cone—black-and-white, of course.

HERE'S WHAT YOU NEED:

- Large sheets of black construction paper
- White construction paper
- A large, round plate or pot lid
- Glue, scissors, and a pencil

HERE'S WHAT YOU DO:

- Using the plate or lid, trace the largest full circle possible on the black paper.
- Cut the circle from the black paper.
- As if cutting a piece of pie, cut out one slice (about an eighth) from your black circle and discard.
- Cut out shapes of small stars from the white paper.
- Glue the stars to the black circle to decorate, staying away from the edges.
- Bring together the edges of the black paper so that they overlap one inch. Then glue the edges, making a cone with the stars on the outside. Let dry.
- Fill with popcorn. Once won't be enough!

> Before your guests leave, fill new cones with black-and-white jelly beans to take home as party favors.

Munchies

CHEEZIE POPCORN

Here's a twist if you're getting bored with just plain butter.

HERE'S WHAT YOU NEED:

- 3 cups popped popcorn
- 3 tablespoons grated Parmesan cheese
- 1 teaspoon salt
- Large brown paper bag

HERE'S WHAT YOU DO:

- While your popcorn is still hot and fresh, place it in the paper bag.
- Add the cheese and salt to the bag.
- Fold the top of the bag over, to seal it completely, and shake vigorously for 45 seconds.
- Pour into your popcorn cones and enjoy!

Experiment with your favorite flavors. Replace the cheese in this recipe with garlic salt, paprika, cumin, heated barbecue sauce, or melted caramel.

STAR SANDWICHES

Here's a fun way to serve your favorite sandwiches:

- Using a large cookie cutter in the shape of a star, cut through a sandwich for a Hollywood snack.
- If you don't have a cookie cutter, cut a piece of cardboard in the shape of a star. Use this as a guide to cut the sandwiches with a sharp knife.

MORE MENU SUGGESTIONS

Serve the Movie Slate Cake or Center Stage Cake (see pages 66 and 68). For breakfast, White Cloud Eggs (page 62) on toast, with orange juice served in champagne glasses, will be a winner.

The Party

The main attraction tonight will be a festival of your favorite films. Start the evening with a hilarious comedy, move into a tearjerker, and doze off during a scary thriller.

YOU BE THE STAR

Take your favorite scene from a movie and act it out! Find a few props or costume pieces around the house, and take turns saying the lines from the film. Can you impersonate the actresses in the movie?

Do they have a special way that they speak or move? Give it a try.

- Find the scene that you want to act out.
- Watch it a few times, and then get in front of the screen yourself. Play the tape, and mouth the words and perform the actions with the actors in the movie providing the soundtrack.
- This is very hard to do without laughing hysterically!

CAN YOU GUESS?

This is a fast-paced game that should be played in teams. Keep score and play until you run out of names!

HERE'S HOW YOU SET UP:

- Cut hundreds of 2- x 1-inch pieces of scrap paper.
- Ask your friends to divide up all the blank pieces of paper and write a famous name on each one.

Names can be of any famous person—living or dead, real or fictional—that all of your guests should recognize.

- Ask your guests to fold the papers in half and place them in a large bowl.

HERE'S HOW YOU PLAY:

- One player picks a name from the bowl and describes the person to her team. The player can say anything except the actual name or letters in the name to get the other team members to correctly identify the celebrity.
- Teams have thirty seconds to guess.
- If a team guesses correctly, it collects the name.
- Names that are not guessed within the time limit are put back in the bowl.
- Teams take turns drawing and guessing names.
- The game is over when there are no slips left in the bowl.
- The team with the most names wins.

Don't forget to return the movies you rented to avoid a late charge!

Hooray for Hollywood!

The Fortune~Teller Party

Palm-print invitations request that your guests RSVP with their birth dates, so that you can prepare party favors that correspond to their astrological signs.

Do you know your sign? Some believe that all people born during the same time of year share similar personality traits, due to the positioning of the stars and the planets at the time of their birth. Each sign has a figure that corresponds to it. Leo is a lion. Pisces is a pair of fish. Do you know the figure for your sign?

A list of astrological birth signs and some qualities of people born under them appears on the next page. See how accurate these are.

Learn how to make a paper fortune-teller for each guest to take home. Play games that use your own psychic abilities, and make your own psychic predictions for the coming year.

Some people believe that the lines in the palms of their hands can foretell the future. Use the chart in this chapter to discover what each line means. Each guest at the party will get her palm read. Can you tell the future?

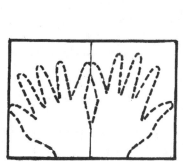

Invitations

• •

Your friends can start reading your palm as soon as they get these invitations!

HERE'S WHAT YOU NEED:

- Sheets of card stock, approximately 8½ x 11 inches
- Ink pad or sponge soaked with washable ink or poster paint
- Pencil and pen or marker
- Scissors
- Envelopes

HERE'S WHAT YOU DO:

- Fold the card stock in half lengthwise to make 5½- x 8½-inch cards.
- Use the pad or sponge to cover your left palm with a thin layer of washable paint or ink.
- For each invitation, press your left hand firmly down on a folded card so that your wrist is at the bottom and the outer edges of your pinkie and palm reach the fold. Press your right fist firmly into the back of your left hand to leave a clear palm print.
- Trace carefully around your outstretched hand with a pencil.
- Cut out the shape of your hand, making sure that you leave some of the fold at the left uncut.
- Open the card, and write your message:

You are invited to Beverly's
Fortune-Teller Sleep-Over!
Come learn about your future!
123 Elm Street, Friday, July 7, at 6 P.M.
RSVP with your birth date, 555-5555

Decorations and Favors

Fill your house with moons, stars, and planets. You can also decorate with the figures and symbols for your guests' astrological signs. When your friends RSVP with their birth dates, use the chart below to figure out their signs.

Make a small scroll on parchment paper for each of your guests, with the figure for her sign and the fortune printed below. Add your own predictions too!

Here are the astrological signs, with the traits, figures, and symbols that apply to them.

Capricorn, December 22 to January 19: You are a very determined person. Once you make up your mind to do something, you stick with it until you get the job done. (The Goat)

Aquarius, January 20 to February 18: You were born under the sign of the genius. You enjoy learning and helping mankind. (The Water Bearer)

Pisces, February 19 to March 20: You are sensitive and poetic. You can easily sense the feelings of other people. (The Fishes)

Aries, March 21 to April 20: You are a leader with undying energy. You don't let anything get in the way of your goal. (The Ram)

Taurus, April 21 to May 20: You like to make great achievements one step at a time. You are a great planner who loves life's comforts. (The Bull)

Gemini, May 21 to June 20: You love to learn new things. You want to know a little bit about everything. (The Twins)

Cancer, June 21 to July 22: You are very caring and family-oriented. Those born under Cancer make the best parents. (The Crab)

Leo, July 23 to August 22: You are a trendsetter, a great performer. You love to be the center of attention. (The Lion)

Virgo, August 23 to September 22: You are a perfectionist. You lead a very organized and exact life. Virgo is also known as the sign of the movie stars! (The Virgin)

Libra, September 23 to October 22: You love beauty and lead a balanced and harmonious life. (The Scales)

Scorpio, October 23 to November 22: If you like something, you *love* it! If you don't like something, you *hate* it! You are very loyal. (The Scorpion)

Sagittarius, November 23 to December 21: You are very playful and love your freedom. You have lofty goals, but you're not a dreamer! (The Archer)

Munchies

· ·

Use the theme of the zodiac to plan your menu. You can serve fried fish for Pisces or steak sandwiches for Taurus, the bull.

> Try the Zodiac Cake (see page 66) decorated with the symbol for your sign.

For breakfast, serve fried eggs to represent the Sun—the ruler of all the planets. Cut apples in half horizontally, to reveal the natural stars that they hide inside.

The Party

· ·

Who knows what tomorrow will bring? Here are a couple of tricks of the trade to help give you insight. Make the fortune-tellers with your friends at the party.

FORTUNE-TELLERS

HERE'S WHAT YOU NEED:

- A square of plain white paper for each guest (8½ x 8½ inches)
- A thin-tip black marker
- Four markers or crayons of different colors

HERE'S WHAT YOU DO:

- Fold all four corners equally to the center of the paper, making a smaller square.
- Flip the paper over and fold the corners in on this side—making an even smaller square.
- Number each of the eight triangles on the inside of your fortune-teller.

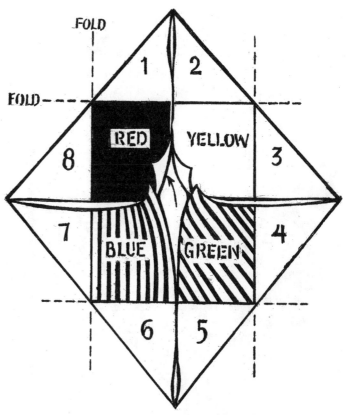

- Open each flap that you have numbered (use two numbers per flap) and write a fortune inside with your black marker.

> Make up your own fortunes and don't show them to your friends, so that every fortune-teller can be unique. Make the fortunes answer questions. For example: YES! IT WILL HAPPEN or NOT LIKELY.

- Flip your fortune-teller over again, and color each of the four outer flaps with solid colors.
- Insert your thumbs and forefingers into each of the colored flaps.
- You are ready to tell the future.

HERE'S HOW YOU PLAY:

- This game is played in pairs. One person is the seer, and the second gets her fortune told.
- The seer holds the paper fortune-teller in her fingers, asking her partner to ask a question and select a color on one of the flaps.

- Once a color is selected, the seer opens and closes the paper, first top to bottom, then side to side. She does this once for each letter of the color her friend has selected. (Three times for "red," for example, because it has three letters.)
- Now the partner is asked to select a number that she sees as she looks into the center of the paper fortune-teller.
- The seer again alternates opening the paper the long and wide ways for the number of times that have been selected.
- Another number is selected, and this time the seer opens up the paper and reads the fortune to answer the question.

26

PALM READING

It is said that your future can be told by reading your palm. Use the chart below to learn the location and meaning of the lines in your hand. Take turns telling the fortunes of your guests—just for fun!

LOVE LINE: Look closely to see if small lines veer off from the main line. This is said to tell the number of people you will fall in love with. If your love line:
- is long, you'll marry someone rich.
- is short, you are very emotional.
- is strong and deep, you are very passionate.

MONEY LINE: If your money line:
- runs to your index finger, you will be rich!
- runs to your middle finger, you'll be succesful in business.
- runs to your little finger, you will inherit lots of money.

Cup your hand slightly. If you see little triangles, that is very lucky!

No matter what your astrological sign is, or the number of lines on your hand, this party should generate some good-hearted fun, optimism for a bright future, and a happy year for everyone at the party.

LIFE LINE: If you look closely, you will see small lines intersecting it. These little lines are said to stand for the major events in your life, including career successes, marriage, and children. If your life line:
- is long and strong, you will live a long and exciting life.
- is short and deep, you'll be very healthy.
- stretches far away from the thumb, you'll be popular and energetic.
- is straight and close to the thumb, you will live a protected life.

The Mystery Party

Here's a great party for girls who love to solve mysteries. Guests receive their invitations in envelopes marked "Top Secret." Each guest will play a part in the Maltese Diamond Mystery, and everyone must come up with an alibi.

The invitations will supply guests with the names of the characters they are to portray at the party. They will pretend to be those people for the entire night.

The setting is a party for a rich heiress. The lights go out, and her diamond disappears! When the lights come back on, you announce that no one is allowed to leave the party until the diamond is recovered.

Can you make up stories as you go along? You need to create a reason why each person would want to steal the diamond!

Invitations

• •

This invitation is a bit more involved than the others in this book. You have to explain that all your guests are to come to the party pretending to be another character from the moment they come in the door.

Decorate the border of the invitation with drawings of diamonds accented with glued-on glitter. Deliver the invite in a brown envelope with the words TOP SECRET written in large black letters.

Here's a suggestion for the text of the invitation:

Mystery Sleep-Over

Help solve the case and play a part!

Everyone will take a role and pretend to be a

suspect in the Maltese Diamond Mystery.

When you arrive at the party, don't use your real

name. Your alias will be *(Insert name of character here, and include explanation of why they might want to steal the diamond—see below)*.

Keep it a secret!

Come dressed for a dinner party as

(name of character)

to the mansion of Miss Viola Upson,

also known as Sara,

123 Elm Street, Friday, January 11, at 6:00 P.M.

RSVP as *(name of character)* 555-5555

Decorations

The opening event of this party is the presentation of the diamond. Create a table covered by flowers. Use a piece of costume jewelry or sculpted tinfoil to represent the priceless diamond.

Decorate your mansion with these beautiful tissue-paper blooms:

TISSUE FLOWERS

HERE'S WHAT YOU NEED:

- Several sheets of colored tissue paper
- Green pipe cleaners
- Scissors

HERE'S WHAT YOU DO:

- Cut five or six 6- x 6-inch squares of tissue paper (use several colors or use multicolored tissue).
- Stack the squares and fold them in an accordion shape.
- Wrap the pipe cleaner tightly around the center of the folded tissue.
- One at a time, open up the tissue papers and fluff them into flowers.

Munchies

At this stylish event, serve finger sandwiches and crackers with cheese on silver platters.

No silver platters? Cut a large oval of sturdy cardboard and cover with tinfoil.

CUCUMBER SANDWICHES

These tiny, elegant sandwiches will go over big with your guests.

HERE'S WHAT YOU NEED:

- 1 large cucumber
- 1 loaf of white bread
- Butter
- Salt

HERE'S WHAT YOU DO:

- Peel the cucumber.
- Cut into round slices, about ¼-inch thick.
- Cut rounds from the bread using a small glass or biscuit cutter.
- Butter and salt the rounds of bread.
- Place a cucumber slice on one round and place another round of bread over the top. Allow about four tea sandwiches for each guest.
- Cover your tray with a lettuce leaf, arrange the tea sandwiches, and serve to your guests.

MORE MENU SUGGESTIONS

Bake the Magnifying Glass Cake (see page 66). For a breakfast treat, eat like an heiress with Cheezie Omelettes (page 61).

The Party

As hostess your role is that of a rich heiress named Viola Upson, who has brought back the huge Maltese Diamond from a recent trip. Viola has invited her friends to a dinner party to show off this newest jewel, which is on display in the "drawing room." Everyone is very interested in the diamond for her own reasons.

Here are some possible characters and motives to assign to your friends when you send out the invitations:

Viola Upson, who wants to claim the insurance money to expand her orchid collection.

Chantal Deval, who wants to satisfy her expensive taste in antique cars.

Lady Hortense Hooplethwaite, who plans to invest in an Amazon emerald mine.

Dame Agatha Huxley, who needs to pay for her orphaned nephew's education.

Madame Dominique Legrand, who wants to repay old gambling debts and start a new life.

Dr. Gertrude Gildersleeve, who has dreams of financing a trek into the desert to explore an Egyptian pharaoh's tomb.

And any others you can think of.

After all your guests arrive, and you've greeted them by their new names, get everyone talking as their character while they eat the cucumber sandwiches in the "drawing room." Before the party starts, choose enough cards from a deck for there to be one per guest; one must be the ace of spades. Now let everyone draw a card, face down. The one who chooses the ace of spades will be the thief, but she must keep it a secret.

Turn out the lights for about a minute, during which time the "thief" will have a chance to steal the diamond and hide it. When the lights come back on, the dia-mond is gone, and everyone is a suspect. Everyone keeps acting like her assigned character, maintaining her innocence, while one by one you and your guests interrogate each other, asking questions that will help to solve the crime.

Each character will be asked a total of twenty-five questions by the group. Choose someone to keep a count of the number of questions asked. After each person has been asked the allotted twenty-five questions, each girl decides for herself who stole the diamond and takes a turn accusing the thief. After everyone has voted, let the real thief come forward!

WHODUNIT?

This is another game you can play to sharpen your detective skills:

HERE'S HOW YOU PLAY:

- Decide who will be the killer by again drawing the ace of spades face down from a deck.
- Tell your guests to go around the room shaking each others' hands. Tell them that if they get two squeezes, they must continue to act normally and shake more hands for five seconds. Then they must stage a very dramatic death and fall on the floor.
- The activity should continue until someone can call out the name of the killer before they get a double squeeze.
- The winner gets to choose the next killer!

Pretending to be a different character can be fun. Remember, the more dramatic you make your performance, the more memorable your party will be.

The Music Video Party

Do you have a favorite music video? Do you know a new dance step? Do you have a secret desire to become a music star one day? This is the perfect party for a group of friends who love music.

Compact-disc-shaped invitations ask your friends to come dressed as their favorite singers and bring music to share.

For the entertainment part of the evening, you and your guests will perform your favorite songs for each other. If you're a true fan, you will know all the words. Lip-synch, or sing along live. Use a camcorder to record all the performances, and then have fun watching the whole tape with your friends and voting who's most likely to become a star.

Make rock T-shirts and a great backdrop with fabric paint. The musical munchie for this party? Spicy drumsticks, of course!

Invitations

These CD invitations set the tone for this toe-tapping slumber party!

HERE'S WHAT YOU NEED:

- Medium-sized coffee can or jar
- Pencil
- Iridescent cellophane
- Glue
- Permanent marker
- Thin cardboard
- Scissors

HERE'S WHAT YOU DO:

- Use a coffee can or jar to trace perfect CD-size circles on the cardboard. Cut out the circles.
- Cover each circle with iridescent cellophane cut to same size and shape.
- Glue down the cellophane.
- Write your invitation message with a permanent marker right on the cellophane:

It's Kari's Music Video Sleep-Over!

Come dressed as your favorite singer, and bring music to share and a plain white T-shirt!

123 Elm Street, Saturday, November 6, at 6:00 P.M.

RSVP 555-5555

Decorations

Music is the theme, so use rock posters and CD jackets to set the mood. Then ask your guests to help create a backdrop for your music video.

Use fabric paints to create a colorful design on an old sheet or piece of canvas or other material. When the paint dries, hang up the backdrop and clear the furniture to get ready for the show!

T-SHIRT DESIGNS

As long as you have fabric paints, why stop with the backdrop? Ask your guests to design their own music-themed T-shirts.

HERE'S WHAT YOU NEED:

- Several bottles and colors of self applicating fabric paint
- Preshrunk T-shirts
- Large cardboard rectangles that are big enough to stretch the T-shirts flat

HERE'S WHAT YOU DO:

- Stretch a T-shirt over a cardboard rectangle.
- Begin painting the shirt, using the cardboard as a hard surface to paint on.
- Experiment with mixing colors and overprinting to create musically inspired original fashions.
- Allow the paint to dry completely overnight, and guests can wear their shirts home the next day!

Munchies

Most top hits have a great beat that makes you want to dance. You can't get the beat without drumsticks. Try these, they're delicious!

SPICY CHICKEN DRUMSTICKS

HERE'S WHAT YOU NEED:

- 24 chicken legs
- ¼ cup oil
- 1 teaspoon salt
- 1 teaspoon black pepper
- 1 small onion
- 2 cloves garlic
- 1 green pepper
- ¼ tablespoon cumin
- 1 tablespoon chili powder
- 1 cup chopped tomatoes
- ¼ cup water

HERE'S WHAT YOU DO:

- Rinse the chicken legs and pat them dry with paper towels.
- Heat the oil in a large pan.
- Shake the salt and black pepper over the chicken legs and brown them on all sides over medium heat, turning often.
- Take the chicken out of the pan and set aside.
- Chop the onion, garlic, and green pepper, and add to the hot pan.
- Stir in the cumin, chili powder, tomatoes, and water.
- Add the browned chicken, and cook for 35 minutes.
- Serves eight.

MORE MENU SUGGESTIONS

Get rocking with a Guitar Cake or Center Stage Cake (pages 67 and 68). And how about using star-shaped bread to make French toast for breakfast?

The Party

With all of your guests dressed like their favorite singers, it's time for a performance.

Your invitation asked that everyone bring music to share. Have your guests select their favorite songs and decide whether to sing out loud or to mouth the words while they do their best to perform for a video camera! Set it all up in front of the backdrop, and move the furniture to make a recording studio.

Make sure that someone knows how to run the camera and that there is a blank tape loaded and ready to record! (Have an extra tape, just in case.) Ask another guest to be in charge of the music, and you might even want to try turning the lights on and off for a special effect.

Draw numbers out of a hat to decide who will perform first, and then roll 'em! Don't be shy. The wilder your performance, the better! When all the performances are complete, pop the tape in the VCR and have fun deciding who has the best moves and star quality!

How well do you know your music? Come up with questions about musical groups and songs to quiz your guests. Offer tapes of your favorite songs as prizes!

Once you get the rhythm going in this party, you'll be jammin' all night long!

The Cowgirl Party

Giddyap, pardners, for a dude-ranch sleep-over. Shine up your boots for one hootin' and hollerin' good-time party!

Saddle-shaped invitations invite guests to a hoedown. Decorate the outside of your house with a life-size scarecrow, to let everyone know where the party is!

Get ready for some great eats! Follow the recipe for a tangy and delicious barbecue sauce that will taste great on your favorite cookout foods.

Create your own country-western line dance while you chow down on some good grub!

Invitations

• •

Saddle up, girls. This invitation will ask all your cowgirl friends to ride on over for the party!

HERE'S WHAT YOU NEED:

• Brown construction paper (8½ x 11 inches)
• Plain white paper (8½ x 11 inches)
• A black marker
• Some string or thin twine
• Scissors, tape, and glue
• Envelopes

HERE'S WHAT YOU DO:

• Cut the brown construction paper and the white paper in half, to end up with four pieces of paper, each measuring 4¼ x 11 inches.
• Fold the paper in half, so that the shorter sections meet evenly.
• Place one white piece of paper inside the brown piece and cut the bottom corners to round them out.
• Cut two inches of string or thin twine, and make a loop that you will tape to the underside of the brown construction paper at the bottom center. You have just made the stirrup for the saddle.
• Glue the white paper to the inside of the construction paper, hiding the ends of the string.
• Use the black marker to create the saddle stitches as shown in the picture.
• Write the invitation information on white paper inside:

Gretta's Slumber Party Hoedown!
Break out your boots and overalls for a rip-roaring good time!
123 Elm Street, Saturday, June 16, at 6:00 P.M.
RSVP 555-5555

Decorations and Favors

Red-and-white checked tablecloths, cowboy boots filled with dried flowers, and cowboy hats filled with bowls of nuts and candy can give your home a country-western feeling.

Add this easy-to-make scarecrow to your front lawn to welcome your guests.

HERE'S WHAT YOU NEED:

- Old jeans or overalls
- A plaid or checked shirt
- Rags
- Rope or twine
- Safety pins
- An old pillowcase
- Straw or hay
- Permanent marking pens
- A straw cowboy hat

HERE'S WHAT YOU DO:

- Stuff rags into the clothes and tie the cuffs of the arms and legs with rope or twine.
- Pin the shirt to the pants.
- Stuff the pillowcase with rags, to make it look like a head. Use markers to draw a face on it.
- Pin the pillowcase to the shirt.
- Stuff straw or hay into the neck of the shirt to give the illusion that the entire scarecrow is stuffed with hay.
- Place the hat on top, and put the scarecrow in front of the house.

> Use bandannas as napkins to add a country look to your table. Have a second set on hand to give away as party favors.

Munchies

Haul out the grill and treat your guests with some down-home barbecue. Use this tangy sauce recipe that goes great on chicken, ribs, and burgers. You'll like it so much that you'll want to dip your fries into it intead of ketchup!

SECRET BARBECUE SAUCE

This recipe makes almost three cups, so you might want to try out a little first, and then make more!

HERE'S WHAT YOU NEED:

- 2½ tablespoons vegetable oil
- 1 small onion, chopped
- 1 clove garlic, minced
- 1 cup ketchup
- ¼ cup cider vinegar
- ½ cup brown sugar
- ⅓ cup Worcestershire sauce
- 1 tablespoon chili powder
- ½ teaspoon cayenne pepper
- 1 tablespoon orange juice

HERE'S WHAT YOU DO:

- Heat the oil in a skillet, and cook the onion and garlic.
- Add all the other ingredients, and mix well over low heat.
- Cover and cook for 20 minutes, stirring occasionally.
- The sauce should get slightly thick.
- Serve as a dipping sauce, or use to season food on the grill.

MORE MENU SUGGESTIONS

Add the Western Boot Cake (page 68) or Guitar Cake (page 67) for a special occasion. Serve granola or Hotta Frittata (page 63) for breakfast as a trail treat.

The Party

Real cowgirls wear silver spurs. You and your guests can make your own to wear with foil and rubber bands.

HERE'S WHAT YOU NEED:

- 1 square foot of foil for each girl
- 2 medium-size rubber bands (tan colored)

HERE'S WHAT YOU DO:

- Cut foil in half.
- Roll each piece until you have formed a snakelike foil rope.
- Slip a rubber band over each shoe or boot just before the ankle.
- Curve the foil around the back of your heel and place the ends into the rubber band on either side of your shoe.

LINE DANCING

What country party would be complete without kicking up your spurs for a little dancing? Country line dancing is easy and fun to do with a group. Teach your friends these simple steps and turn up the music!

HERE'S WHAT YOU DO:

Stand side-by-side in a line, and follow these steps:

- Walk forward, leading with your right foot, for three steps, and touch your left foot to the right on the fourth beat.
- Walk backward, leading with your left foot, for three steps, and touch your right foot together with the left on the fourth beat.
- Step to the side with the right foot and bring the left foot to meet the right foot, then repeat.

- Step to the side with the left foot and bring the right foot to meet the left foot, then repeat.
- Do the first step again: Walk forward, leading with your right foot for three steps, and touch your left foot together with the right on the fourth beat.
- Step forward on your right foot and pivot your body one-quarter turn and bring both feet together.

Repeat this dance until you come back to where you started.

When you have mastered this dance, add turns and variations to make up your own line dance.

Y'all come back next year, ya hear?!

The Treasure Hunt Party

Your treasure chest invitations reveal that hundreds of years ago a band of pirates came to your town and hid their treasure!

Hidden clues bring guests through a whole evening of searching. Everyone gets a head kerchief—just like a pirate—to get in the right mood. Make a delicious pirate punch for your guests, because looking for hidden treasure can make you very thirsty. Have some more party fun by playing a game called Walk the Plank!

Just before bed it's time to tell a scary pirate story that everyone makes up together. The next morning share doubloon pancakes before splitting up the booty.

Invitations

•••••••••••••••••••••••••••••••

In the shape of a treasure chest, this invitation sets the mood for an adventure party!

HERE'S WHAT YOU NEED:

- White construction paper
- Markers
- Gold glitter
- Scissors and glue

HERE'S WHAT YOU DO:

- Fold the bottom third of the paper up toward the top.
- Fold the top third toward the bottom of the paper.
- With scissors, round off the top corners, cutting completely through the paper.
- With a black marker, draw lines, rivets, and a lock.

Open the invitation to write your message. Accent with gold glitter to represent the treasure you will be searching for:

It's Katy's Treasure Hunt Sleep-Over!
We have discovered a 200-year-old map!
Come help search for buried treasure left behind by pirates!
123 Elm Street, Saturday, August 11, at 5:30 P.M.
RSVP 555-5555

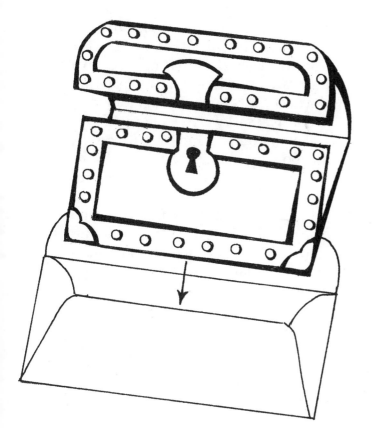

Decorations and Favors

. . . .

PIRATE FLAGS

Every ship stakes its claim with a colorful flag. Make a few to give your party the feel of the high seas.

HERE'S WHAT YOU NEED:

- An old white sheet
- Scissors
- Permanent marker
- Clothesline (optional)

HERE'S WHAT YOU DO

- Cut sheet into several large rectangles.
- Decorate with markers. (Try pirate symbols, stripes, and other patterns.)
- Display on the clothesline or hang individually.

Kerchiefs that can be worn pirate-style make dandy party favors. Or you can encourage your friends to come wearing eye patches or other buccaneer gear.

TREASURE HUNT

Your main preparation will be in creating and setting up the treasure hunt. You need to write twelve clues that will lead your guests to twelve different locations. Decide whether the locations will be around your house or in your neighborhood, and whether they will be inside or outside.

You can use the same pattern as the invitation to write your clues on. Hide them in twelve different places, and let each one lead to the next. Don't set the clues up too early, in case someone stumbles upon one by accident. Make sure that they are in a secure place that is not too obvious.

The clues should be a little difficult to figure out, but not so hard that your guests never find the treasure! It's fun to make the clues rhyme. Here are some examples:

If you have a big old oak tree in your backyard, you might want to write this clue: *For riches bright and riches gold—go to the oak that's very old!*

If you want to hide a clue near your mailbox, try this clue: *For twenty years our ship set sail—now find a clue where you get mail.*

Guests can get to the first clue with the help of the pirate map that you "discovered." Actually, you will make the map by using markers or crayons on parchment paper.

Draw some landmarks (a tree, a swing set, your mailbox), and mark the spot where the first clue is with an X. Once the map is drawn, roll it up, crinkle it, and fold it, so that it looks as though it is two hundred years old.

The twelfth clue will lead your guests to the treasure. It can be an old box that is sealed up securely with tape and rope. Together you and your guests can rip it open to reveal the "treasure."

The treasure can be anything you want—chocolate-chip cookies, gold-foil chocolate coins, necklaces that you have strung yourself with beads, old costume jewelry, balloons, puzzle books, or anything else that would be fun to give your guests as party favors to take home.

> Make sure you have enough treasure for every one of your guests. You don't want to hurt anyone's feelings by running out of loot!

Munchies

Searching for treasure can make a person very thirsty. Here's a great punch to pick you up!

PIRATE PUNCH

HERE'S WHAT YOU NEED:

- 2 ice-cube trays
- 2 dozen seedless green grapes
- 1 liter cranberry juice
- 1 liter cherry juice
- 1 liter ginger ale
- 1 bag of frozen pitted cherries
- Punch bowl

HERE'S WHAT YOU DO:

- Place one grape into each ice cube compartment, fill with cranberry juice, and place in freezer.
- Pour the cherry juice, ginger ale, and any remaining cranberry juice into the punch bowl.
- Add the cherries.
- Chill punch in the refrigerator until ready to serve.
- Just before serving, place several of the grape ice cubes into glasses and fill with punch.

MORE MENU SUGGESTIONS

Share the Hidden Treasure Cake (page 68) with your pirate pals. Doubloon Pancakes (page 62) for breakfast are worth their weight in gold.

The Party

When all your guests have arrived, show them the pirate map and begin your hunt. Go from clue to clue until you reach the treasure! To celebrate your discovery, try these fun games too!

WALK THE PLANK

HERE'S WHAT YOU NEED:

- Duct tape
- A soup spoon
- 6 hard-boiled eggs

HERE'S WHAT YOU DO:

- Run a straight line of duct tape on the ground for ten feet.
- One by one, take turns balancing a hard-boiled egg on the end of the spoon while you walk all the way across the taped line—without losing your balance or dropping the egg!

SCARY STORY

This is a great game to play right before bedtime when it's very dark outside. All you need is a flashlight.

HERE'S HOW YOU PLAY:

- Sit in a circle, with the lights turned low to add to the eerie effect.
- Decide who will start the game. That person shines the flashlight under her chin and begins the story with the words: "It was a dark and stormy night. . . ."
- The flashlight is then quickly passed to the person on her immediate left.
- The new person shines the flashlight on her face and adds only one word to the story before passing the flashlight to the next girl on her immediate left.

- Each player adds on to the story one word at a time—very quickly—until you have created one big scary story.
- If a player waits too long or if her word doesn't make sense—she is out!
- Can you finish the story without losing a single player?

· ·

This party is full of treasures, and it's fun to share them with your friends.

The Talent Show Party

Can you balance a pencil on your nose? Can you cluck like a chicken? Can you count backward from one hundred in Portuguese? No matter what your hidden talent, this party is for the performer in you.

It's a sleep-over talent show! You may be surprised at your friends' hidden talents. Casting-call invitations ask guests to come prepared to perform. Popcorn-ball microphone snacks give guests the energy to perform their best.

Follow the directions to make medals for all of your guests to wear around their necks and take home. Everyone's a winner in this contest—everyone gets a prize.

What's your hidden talent? Now's your chance to shine!

Invitations

It's time to dust off those tap shoes and warm up those vocal cords. Tell all your friends to practice their acts!

Calling All Stars!
Come perform at Cecily's Talent Show Sleep-Over!
Let's share our talent just for fun!
Come dressed to perform.
123 Elm Street, Saturday, March 6, at 6:00 P.M.
RSVP 555-5555

Decorations and Favors

In this talent competition, everyone's a winner. Each of your guests will receive a medal for her efforts. While you follow the directions to make these medals, think of all the categories you can award in your talent show.

HERE ARE A FEW SUGGESTIONS:

- Most Imaginative Costume
- Funniest Talent
- Best Shoes
- Best Act with a Guitar and Tap Shoes
- Best Use of Confetti and Jell-O

CHAMPIONSHIP MEDALS

HERE'S WHAT YOU NEED:

- Gold ribbon
- Scissors
- Cardboard
- A juice glass
- Foil (tin or colored)
- Hole punch

HERE'S WHAT YOU DO:

- Cut enough ribbon to fit over your head.
- Use the juice glass to trace a circle on the cardboard that will be the medal.
- Cut the circle out of the cardboard.
- Cover the cardboard circle with foil.
- Punch a hole near the edge of the foil-covered circle, thread the ribbon through, and tie.

Make a medal for everyone at your talent show. There are no losers in this competition.

SET THE STAGE

Set up chairs in front of a large open area—and there's your stage! Be sure to have a backstage area where a performer can't be seen by the audience, in case you have any acts that require the element of surprise.

Ask your guests to wear their cosutmes to the party to save time. You want them to be completely prepared to perform at their best.

Munchies

• •

It will be hard to resist singing your favorite tunes into these popcorn-ball microphones: They're almost as much fun to play with as they are to eat!

POPCORN-BALL MICROPHONES

HERE'S WHAT YOU NEED:

- 10 cups freshly popped popcorn (no salt or butter)
- 2 cups light corn syrup
- 1 tablespoon cider vinegar
- ½ teaspoon salt
- 1 tablespoon vanilla
- Wax paper
- Empty paper towel rolls, cut in half

HERE'S WHAT YOU DO:

- Mix corn syrup, salt, and vinegar in a large pot over medium heat until thick.
- Add vanilla.
- Place warm, fresh popcorn in a large bowl.
- Pour syrup mixture over the popcorn, as you stir constantly to coat almost every kernel.
- Let cool a little, but as soon as you can touch the mixture without burning yourself, roll it into 4-inch balls. Place them on wax paper to cool completely.
- Stick a paper towel roll in the end, and you have a handle for your microphone!

MORE MENU SUGGESTIONS

Take a bow with the Center Stage Cake on page 68. A serving of Hotta Frittata (page 63) will keep the energy up.

The Party

Write numbers on little pieces of paper and place them in a hat. Make one number for each guest at your party. Whoever selects number 1 will be the first performer.

Have each guest write down the name of her act on a piece of paper. Select one person to be the Mistress of Ceremonies who will introduce each act. Encourage your audience to give lots of support and applause to their fellow performers.

You might even be able to have some of the guests perform twice or together. The goal is *not* to compete for being the most talented person at the party, but to enjoy everyone's talents and have fun together.

After the performances, it is time to hand out medals to everyone. Make a big ceremony of placing a medal on each guest and making her feel good. Everyone is a winner!

The Princess Party

It's your party, so you can be anyone you'd like to be. Why not a princess? Of course, you will want the other princesses from all the surrounding kingdoms to come to your castle to help you celebrate.

A drawbridge invitation requests that your friends come dressed in royal garb. You'll decorate your castle with fairy princess magic wands that your guests can take home as party favors.

What does a princess do with all the frogs she kisses who don't turn into princes? Serve them for dinner, of course! Here is a fantastic recipe for Faux Frog Legs! Yum! (Don't worry: *Faux*, pronounced *foe*, means "fake"—these frog legs are just chicken!)

Creating a royal wishbook, making magic necklaces, and playing Princess-Hat Ring Toss are highlights of this royal gala.

Invitations

· ·

The drawbridge is being lowered for your party—so here are drawbridge invitations to let all the princesses know about it.

HERE'S WHAT YOU NEED:

- Yellow construction paper
- Brown construction paper
- Scissors and glue
- Markers or crayons

HERE'S WHAT YOU DO:

- Cut yellow construction paper into rectangles measuring 4¼ x 11 inches.
- Cut out two squares across the top of the paper to look like the top of a castle.
- Fold the bottom of the paper up, one inch from the top.
- In the flap that you folded up, cut the corners to round them off and cut away one-half inch from either side of the flap—stopping at the fold.
- Trace the rounded front flap onto the brown construction paper.
- Cut out the piece you have traced and glue it on the flap to become the drawbridge.
- Write your invitation message behind the drawbridge door:

Hear Ye! Hear Ye!
All Princesses Throughout the Land!
Come to Princess Lisa's Sleep-Over Party!
123 Elm Street, Friday, May 30, at 6:00 P.M.
RSVP 555-5555

Decorations and Favors

It is a well-known fact that many princesses possess magic powers. What you might not know is that none of their powers would work without their magic wands! You can make these wands at your party with the other princesses, or prepare them ahead of time to decorate the castle before the guests arrive. Make enough wands so that everyone can take one home.

HERE'S WHAT YOU NEED:

- Unsharpened pencils
- Glue
- A shoe box
- Silver glitter
- Cardboard
- Scissors

HERE'S WHAT YOU DO:

- Smear glue over the entire surface of an unsharpened pencil.
- Drop the pencil into the shoe box and sprinkle it with silver glitter, making sure to cover it completely.
- Cut a star shape out of the cardboard, cover it with glue, and sprinkle the star with glitter as well.
- When both the star and the pencil have dried completely, glue or tape the star to one end of the pencil.
- Store the completed wands star-side up, so that their magic doesn't run out.

Munchies

. . . .

They say princesses may have to kiss a few frogs before they find Prince Charming. What to do with the rejects? Here's a great idea:

FAUX FROG LEGS (CHICKEN)

HERE'S WHAT YOU NEED:

- 2 pounds skinless, boneless chicken breasts
- One cup flour, with salt and black pepper to taste
- 2 eggs, beaten
- One cup bread crumbs
- One cup grated Parmesan cheese
- Nonstick spray
- Cookie sheet

HERE'S WHAT YOU DO:

- Wash the chicken and pat it dry with paper towels.
- Cut chicken into half-inch strips.
- Roll strips in flour, salt, and pepper mixture, and shake to remove excess.
- Shake strips into beaten egg, coating completely.
- Roll strips into mixture of bread crumbs and Parmesan cheese.
- Place them on cookie sheet that is coated with nonstick spray.
- Bake at 400° for 10 minutes, or until golden.
- Turn the "legs" over, and bake them for 10 more minutes, or until you can insert a fork into the meat easily, and any juice runs clear.
- Serve in sets of four legs!

MORE MENU SUGGESTIONS

Bake a Castle Cake (page 69) for all your royal friends. White Cloud Eggs (page 62) for breakfast will taste heavenly.

The Party

. . . .

When all the princesses have arrived, distribute the magic wands or make them together. Now it is time for the princesses to begin their wish-making.

ROYAL WISHBOOK

HERE'S WHAT YOU NEED:

- A small blank notebook or autograph book
- Magic wands

HERE'S WHAT YOU DO:

- Before the party, decorate the cover with your favorite colors and designs.

- During the party, each princess must make a wish for each of the other princesses. Then the princesses can each wish for something for themselves.
- Write all your wishes in the Royal Wishbook.
- Ask all your princesses to wave their magic wands for good luck.

If you prefer, why not inscribe your royal wishes in the Memory Book section that follows page 70?

MAGIC NECKLACES

After the wishing is over, you might want to make some magic necklaces with the princesses.

HERE'S WHAT YOU NEED:

- Tinfoil
- A sewing needle
- Strong thread

HERE'S WHAT YOU DO:

- Take small strips of tinfoil and fold them into small squares. Do not fold them too tightly, or you will not be able to string them.
- With a needle and strong thread, carefully thread the foil squares and string as many as you like.

Be very careful with the needle. The point is very sharp. Sit at a table while you are making these necklaces, and ask an adult to help.

- Make sure that the string is long enough to fit over your head.
- Tie the ends of the string and wear!

PRINCESS-HAT RING TOSS

Use an 11- x 17-inch piece of colored construction paper to create a cone-shaped hat secured with tape or glue. Twist together two pipe cleaners into a circle. One guest wears the hat, holding it firmly as the others take turns tossing the pipe cleaner circles onto it. The princess with the most successful tosses wins.

With all this royal fun, your guests won't want to return to their own castles.

Breakfast

Did you get any sleep? Here are some great morning meals to share with your guests before they leave your party.

Cheezie Omelettes

This makes one large omelette. Cut into pieces and share. Make as many omelettes as you need.

HERE'S WHAT YOU NEED:

- 1 tablespoon butter or margarine
- 3 medium or 2 large eggs per guest
- 1 tablespoon milk
- ¼ cup grated cheese (your favorite kind)

HERE'S WHAT YOU DO:

- Melt the butter in a skillet at medium-high heat.
- Scramble the eggs and milk in a small bowl.
- Pour the egg-and-milk mixture into the skillet. Allow the eggs to cover the entire surface of the pan.
- When the eggs have set, sprinkle the cheese throughout.
- With a spatula, fold one side of the omelette on top of the other, creating a half circle with the cheese inside.
- Flip the half circle over, to cook evenly, and slide onto a plate.
- Serve.

French Toast

HERE'S WHAT YOU NEED:

- 4 eggs
- ⅓ cup milk
- 1½ tablespoons sugar
- 1 teaspoon cinnamon
- 2 tablespoons butter or margarine
- 6 slices of French bread, cut on an angle
- Syrup
- Powdered sugar
- Fresh fruit

HERE'S WHAT YOU DO:

- Beat the eggs with a fork in a medium-size bowl.
- Add milk, sugar, and cinnamon to the eggs until mixed well.
- Melt butter in a frying pan over medium heat.
- Dip the bread in the egg mixture, coating both sides.
- Carefully brown both sides of the bread in the frying pan.
- Serve with syrup, powdered sugar, or fresh fruit.

White Cloud Eggs

HERE'S WHAT YOU NEED:

- 1 tablespoon vinegar
- 2 eggs per guest
- ½ teaspoon salt
- Toasted bread

HERE'S WHAT YOU DO:

- Fill a large skillet a little more than half full of water.
- Add the vinegar, and bring the water to a simmer.
- Break the eggs, one at a time, onto a small plate, being careful not to break the yolk. If your pot is small you may need to do this in batches.
- Slide the eggs gently into the simmering water.
- Add a pinch of salt to the water.
- With a spoon, keep covering the eggs with the water until eggs are set.
- You know the eggs are done when the whites become solid.
- Slide the eggs onto the toasted bread and serve.

Doubloon Pancakes

HERE'S WHAT YOU NEED:

- ¾ cup milk
- 1 egg
- 2 tablespoons butter, melted
- 1 cup flour
- 2 tablespoons sugar
- 2 teaspoons baking powder
- ⅛ teaspoon salt
- Nonstick cooking spray
- Syrup
- Fresh fruit

HERE'S WHAT YOU DO:

- Blend milk, egg, and butter in a medium bowl.
- Mix flour, sugar, baking powder, and salt in another bowl.
- Blend the wet and dry ingredients together.
- Coat frying pan with cooking spray or more butter, and sizzle over medium heat.
- Spoon out batter to make 4-inch-wide pancakes. Flip them over when the batter bubbles.

- Serve these golden doubloons with syrup or fresh fruit.
- Serves six.

Hotta Frittata

HERE'S WHAT YOU NEED:

- 3 tablespoons oil
- 1 small onion, chopped
- 6 eggs
- ¼ cup chopped tomatoes and mushrooms
- ½ cup cheddar cheese
- Salt and black pepper

HERE'S WHAT YOU DO:

- Heat the oil in a large skillet.
- Add the onion, and cook until transparent.
- In a medium bowl, scramble the eggs and mix in the tomatoes, mushrooms, and cheese.
- Pour the egg mixture into the skillet.
- Cover and cook for 3 to 4 minutes.
- Sprinkle the top with salt and pepper.
- Serve in wedges—like a pizza.
- Serves six to eight.

Cakes

• •

Cakes help to celebrate all kinds of parties. If it is your birthday, add candles and sing the song! If you're celebrating a different occasion— just dig in!

All these cakes correspond to the themes of the parties in this book. Use your favorite recipe or boxed mix. Choose the cake that you think will add the right flavor to your celebration.

Camera Cake

• •

For this camera-shaped cake you will need one prepared 9- x 13-inch rectangular, unfrosted cake and one 8-inch round cake. The cake should be your favorite flavor. Use a mix or follow your own favorite recipe.

HERE'S WHAT YOU NEED:

- 9- x 13-inch unfrosted cake
- 8-inch round unfrosted cake
- 1 cup butter or margarine
- ¼ teaspoon salt
- 6 cups confectioners' sugar
- 6 tablespoons of milk
- Cake decorating icing (one or two colors)

HERE'S WHAT YOU DO:

- Using an electric mixer, cream together the salt and butter in a large bowl.
- With a spoon, mix in the confectioners' sugar one cup at a time.
- Between cups of sugar, add a tablespoon of milk until all the sugar and milk are added to the frosting mixture.
- When the cakes are completely cool, take the rectangular cake and cut 2 inches off the end with sharp knife. Now your cake will measure 9 x 11 inches.
- Cut a 2- x 2-inch square from the strip you just cut off. Place the square above the upper right hand corner of the rectangular cake.
- Frost the top and sides of the rectangular cake including the added 2- x 2-inch square as if it is attached.

- Place the 8-inch round cake centered on top of the rectangular cake.
- Frost the top and sides of the round cake.
- With your favorite color (or colors) of cake decorating icing, add lines and any message.

Movie Slate Cake

In the shape of a movie slate, this cake leaves no question who the star is of this party.

Here's What You Need:

- One large sheet cake, frosted white
- Cake decorating icing, or a pastry bag with a thin tip filled with chocolate frosting.
- Cake decorating icing, or a pastry bag with a thin tip filled with red frosting.

Here's What You Do:

- Use the chocolate decorating icing to create the lines in the illustration to represent a movie slate board. Carefully create the stripes of the top clapper.
- With the red decorating icing, fill in the following information:
  MOVIE: SLEEPOVER
  STARRING: (*WRITE YOUR NAME HERE*)
- Lights! Camera! Action! Serve!

Zodiac Cake

Is there an artist in your family? If not, trace a picture of the figure for your sign, and use it as a pattern to decorate a cake, whether round or square, one layer or two, chocolate or vanilla. Or make a circle using all twelve signs.

Use red frosting to make the crab for Cancer. Use lots of pretty colors against blue frosting to make the Pisces fish. Be creative—the results will be delicious.

Magnifying Glass Cake

Here's What You Need:

- One 5- x 5-inch square cake (any flavor)
- One 9-inch round cake (any flavor)
- 2 cups chocolate icing
- ½ cup light blue or white icing

Guitar Cake

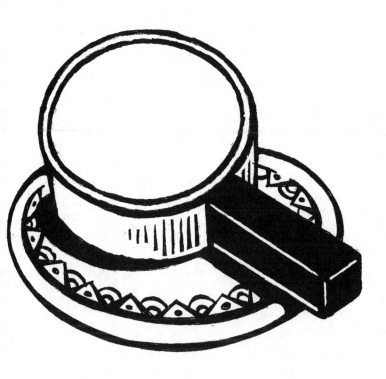

HERE'S WHAT YOU NEED:

- Two 9-inch round cake layers (any flavor)
- One 9- x 9-inch square cake layer (any flavor)
- 3 cups frosting
- Decorating Icing

HERE'S WHAT YOU DO:

- Place the round cake layers side by side. These will make up the body of the guitar.
- With a serrated knife, carefully cut a raindrop shape from the right end of the right cake layer. Remove this part.
- Cut curves in the points that you have created.
- Cut the square cake into rectangles, each 3 inches wide and 9 inches long.
- Place the rectangles end-to-end, to create the neck of the guitar coming out of the area where you cut out the raindrop shape.
- Frost the neck in a different color from the body. Be creative with your design and use several colors.
- Use the decorating icing to make strings.

HERE'S WHAT YOU DO:

- Cut the square cake in half and place the two short ends together, to make the handle of the magnifying glass (10 inches long and 2½ inches wide).
- Place the round cake at the top of the handle.
- With chocolate icing, frost the entire handle and the edges of the round cake.
- Use the light blue or white icing to frost the top of the round cake.
- Write your own message on the round cake.

Western Boot Cake

HERE'S WHAT YOU NEED:

- One large sheet cake
- 3 cups frosting
- Cake decorating icing

HERE'S WHAT YOU DO:

- Cut the cake into two boot shapes opposite each other (one upside down) as in the picture.
- Frost the top and sides of the cakes.
- Use the cake decorating icing to add lines representing stitching on Western-style boots.
- Serve both boots together.

Hidden Treasure Cake

The cake can be any flavor and shape that you want. The treasure in this cake is hidden inside!

Once you have poured the cake batter into the pans, add candies that will be baked right inside as "treasures." Use jellied or gummy animal candies or M&M's to add a treasure surprise to the cake that looks normal from the outside!

> Although any flavor of cake will work, white, vanilla, or lemon cake will make the treasures stand out more!

Center Stage Cake

Whether you have a Makeover, Hollywood, Music Video, or Talent Show party, this cake is a winner.

HERE'S WHAT YOU NEED:

- One large sheet cake (any flavor)
- 2 cups white frosting
- 1 cup red frosting
- 1 cup chocolate icing or packaged decorating icing

HERE'S WHAT YOU DO:

- Use the white frosting to cover the sheet cake smoothly and completely.
- Use the red frosting to create cur-

tains that are pulled back at either end of your cake.

- Make a top border of red scallops between the two curtains. (This is known as a "teaser" curtain.)
- Use the chocolate frosting to make footlights across the bottom of your cake—they look like little thumbs.
- Write your own message center stage.

Castle Cake

• •

This sheet cake is easy to decorate, and it looks just like a castle when you're done!

HERE'S WHAT YOU NEED:

- One large sheet cake (any flavor)
- 2 cups white frosting
- Chocolate decorating icing
- Green decorating icing
- Red decorating icing
- Toothpicks
- Blue construction paper
- Scissors and glue

HERE'S WHAT YOU DO:

- Cut away the top of the cake, according to the pattern shown in the picture, to make the top of the castle.
- Use the white frosting to cover the cake, smoothing the frosting out evenly with a butter knife.
- Use a knife to make horizontal indentations in the white frosting. These represent the mortar lines of the castle's stones.
- Use a toothpick to create the alternating vertical stone lines.
- Use chocolate decorating icing to create a drawbridge in the center of the castle.
- Use the green decorating icing to make a border of grass growing along the bottom of the cake.
- Use the red decorating icing to write a message.
- Cut small blue triangles from the construction paper and glue them to toothpicks to create pennants flying from the castle roof.
- Serve to your royal guests.

Memory Book

One great way to remember your sleepover is to create your own memory book. This book will become a keepsake.

HERE'S WHAT YOU NEED:

- Pull-out section at the back of this book
- Hole punch
- 32-inch length of ribbon

HERE'S WHAT YOU DO:

- Cut out pages along dotted line.
- Punch three holes where marked.
- Thread the ribbon through the holes as shown. Gently pull the ribbon taut. Make a bow to tie it off.
- Use the inside pages for pictures, autographs, and stories. Make up headings like "Who Was There," "What We Did," "The Funniest Thing That Happened," and so on.

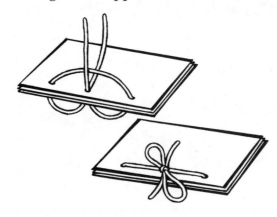